M

30 DAYS - The Workbook

MARC REKLAU

30 DAYS - The Workbook

MARC REKLAU

30 DAYS - The Workbook

MARC REKLAU

30 DAYS - The Workbook

NOTES:

93. Get a coach!

Action Step:
If you have any questions contact me at marc@marcreklau.com, or apply for a 30-minutes Strategy Session with me.

94. Live your life fully. Do it NOW!

Action Step:

Do the things you always wanted to do NOW. Make plans NOW!

List 5 things you always wanted to do and set a date:

1. _____ Date: _____
2. _____ Date: _____
3. _____ Date: _____
4. _____ Date: _____
5. _____ Date: _____

92. Things are only temporary

Action Step:
Think back on other hard times in your life and how you got out of it and maybe even found something positive in it after some time.

Exercise:
<u>MAPPING LIFE</u>
1. Make a Timeline of your life. From birth to now. Mark every key event of your life on
    the line. Moments that changed your life.

2. Write the great moments, the successes above the timeline

3. Write the challenges, the tragedies, the failures below the timeline

4. Examine the events below the line and write the positive effects of them above the
    line.

(For example somebody close died. A positive effect could be that you value your life more;
 or you got fired from a job, but this opened doors for an even better job that you have now)

91. What price are you paying for NOT changing?

Power Questions:

1) Are you paying a price for doing the same old thing?

2) What is it?

3) What will you do about it?

90. Step out of your "comfort zone"

Power Questions:
1) How can you challenge yourself to step out of your comfort zone? (Remember: small steps)

2) Is there anything that makes you uncomfortable you can do NOW?

89. Have a highlight every day

Action Step:
Celebrate something every day: A good job at work, life!
Call a friend, Take somebody for lunch, Get a Massage, Go for a drink, Go to the movies/theater/a concert, Get a Manicure or pedicure, Movie night at Home, Watch a sunrise,...
Don't forget to reserve some time for your special moments in your schedule!

88. Take Time off

Power Questions:

What will you do less of?

When will you take some time off?

Action Step:

Schedule some relaxation time in your calendar right now!

86. Don't be the slave of your phone

Action step:
Try it out! Don't take every call and leverage voicemail.

87. How to deal with problems

Action Step:
Make a list of the problems you have in your life right now that you haven't found a solution for yet. Start working on them.

Power Questions:
What would change if you see this problems as challenges or even opportunities? How would it make you feel?

84. Use your travel time wisely

Power Questions:
Will you use your travel time better?

What will you do?

When will you start?

Action Step:
Do it for two weeks and tell me how your life changed.

85. Spend more time with your family

Power Questions:
How and where are you going to find more time for your family? (Use the tips from this book)

What will you stop doing to find more time?

83. No worries

Action steps:
1) Make a list of your worries:

2) Now categorize them:
- Worries related to the past
- Worries about the future
- Worries outside of your control
- Worries you can actually do something about

3) Forget all of the worries of the first three categories and work on the rest: those that are in your control and not related to the future, the past or our of your control!

81. The power of Meditation

Action Step:
Start meditating for 10-20 minutes a day

82. Listen to great music – daily!

Action Steps:
Write down your 5 favorite songs of all times here:

1._____

2._____

3._____

4._____

5._____

Make a playlist on your iPod, phone or PC and listen to them right now! Do it NOW! Come on!

Power Questions:
How did you feel after listening to your favorite songs? Any changes in your mood?

What would happen if you make this a daily habit? Why not do this for the next 30 days every day?

80. Solve your problems, even if you didn't cause them

Power Questions:
How can you be different?

What can you do different?

What can YOU do to solve the problem?

Action steps:
1) Make a list of all your problems and start working on their solutions.
2) Examine your problems.
3) Look for patterns (Do the same things happen to you over and over again?)

79. A random act of kindness every day

Action Step:
Commit yourself to doing one random act of kindness a day for the next 2 weeks.
Observe what happens, but don't expect anything in return!

Write down some things you could do here:

77. Enjoy more

Action Step:
Remind yourself to be more in the present moment!
(My friend David wears his wristwatch on the right arm. This reminds him to be in the present moment whenever he watches his left arm for the time and notices it's not there.)

Power Questions:
What can you do to be more present?

78. Stop judging!

Action Step:
Make a list of what bothers you most about others. Examine it. Can you learn something from it? Is it a characteristic you have, or you had? Or is it one you want?

74. Treat your body like the temple it is!

Action Step:
What will you do now to have a healthier lifestyle? Write at least 3 things:

1._____

2._____

3._____

75. Exercise at least 3 times a week

Action steps:
1) Find some studies about the amazing benefits of exercising on the internet.

2) When will YOU start exercising: **SET A DATE AND STICK TO IT**:_____

3) If you think you don't have time go back to the chapters on Time Management and find time!

76. Take action. Make things happen

Action Step:
What will you start TODAY?

73. Pamper yourself

Action Step:
Write a list of 15 things that you can do to spoil yourself and then do one of them every other day for the next two weeks. This exercise is truly miraculous! (Examples: read a good book, go to the movies, get a massage, watch a sunrise, sit by the water etc.) Once you start treating yourself well this will do miracles for your self-confidence and self-esteem! Start doing it NOW!

1) _____

2) _____

3) _____

4) _____

5) _____

6) _____

7) _____

8) _____

9) _____

10) _____

11) _____

12) _____

13) _____

14) _____

15) _____

72. Be your authentic self

Power Questions:
1) On a scale form 0-10 how would you quantify your level of authenticity?

2) How many roles do you play?

3) Who are you when you are alone?

4) When was the last time you felt authentic?

5) What will you do from to day on to become more authentic?

71. Stop being so hard on yourself

Action Steps:
1) Accept yourself as you are!
2) Forgive yourself! Love yourself!
3) Take extremely good care of yourself!

Power Questions:
In what areas of your life re you being too hard on yourself?

What benefits do you get from it?

70. Your best investment

Power Question:
What are you going to do? Remember baby steps count, too!

Action Step:
Write down what you commit to in the next 12 months:

I, _____
will read __ book(s) a month,
listen to __ learning CDs or audiobooks per month,
sign up for __ training(s) in the next six months

Date: _____
Signature: _____

68. Live your own life

Action Step:
In what aspect are you not living your life right now? Make a list!

69. Who is number one?

Action Step:
Use at least one of the following exercises to boost your self confidence:

1) Journaling Exercise (Chapter 64)
2) Make a list of successes and achievements
3) Make a list of all the things you are doing great
4) Mirror exercise (Tell yourself how great you are in front of a mirror!- it might feel strange at first, but you'll get used to it)

67. Stop spending time with the wrong people!

Action Steps:
1. Make a list of all the persons you have in your life and are spending time with. (Members of your family, friends, colleagues).

2. Analyze who is positive for you and who drags you down.

3. Spend more time with the positive people and stop seeing the toxic people (blamers, complainers) in your life - or at least spend less time with them.

4. Choose to be around positive people who support you

5. Watch Steve Jobs' Stanford commencement address

66. Become a receiver!

Action Steps:
1) From now on just say "Thank you!" for every gift and compliment you get! (Don't explain or justify.)

2) Analyze if you have any of the five behaviors mentioned in the book. If yes - work on it/them.

Write down your thoughts on this exercise:

65. Stop whining!

Action Steps:
1) Make a list of all your complaints

2) Next to each complain on the list write what it has achieved

3) Transform your complaints into requests.

63. Listen to your inner voice

Action step:
Reread the chapter and find ways to practice listening to your inner voice.

64. Write into your journal

Action step:
Answer the following questions every night before sleeping and write them into your journal:

- What am I grateful for? (Write 3-5 points)
- What 3 things have made me happy today?
- What 3 things did I do particularly well today?
- How could I have made today even better?
- What is my most important goal for tomorrow?

61. Change your posture

Action Steps:
Watch the TED-Talk of Amy Cuddy!

Do the Power Posture at least two minutes a day for a week

62. Ask for what you really want

Action Steps:
Write a list of all the things that you want and don't ask for.

Start asking. Work on it.

59. Do it now!

Power Questions:
What are you procrastinating?

Are you productive or just being busy?

What is really important right now?

60. Fake it till you make it

Power Questions:
Which quality do you want?

How would you act if you already had that quality?

How would you speak, walk, behave, etc.?

58. Accept your emotions

Power Question:
Can you spot a "negative" emotion?

Which symptoms do you feel and in which part of your body?

How do you feel? Be precise!

Action step:
Explore!
Permit the expression of the emotion and analyze what provoked it.
Remember: Emotions are not good or bad. They just are.

30 DAYS - The Workbook

56. Keep expectations low and then shine

Power Questions
In which areas of your life are you promising too much and then have to struggle to keep your promise?

Action Step:
This coming week under-promise on everything..and then over-deliver!

57. Design your ideal day

Action Step:
Bring your ideal day to life!
Write down exactly how you would like your ideal life to be:

53. The Power of Affirmations

Action Step:
Write down at least one affirmation that you will repeat for the next 30 days:

1._____

2._____

3._____

54. Write it down 25 times a day

Power Question:
What is your wish that you will write down 25 times a day from today until you have it? (Use an extra journal)

55. Stop making excuses

Power Questions:
What are you going to choose from now on? Excuses or focused action?

What are the excuses you are using to not change?

51. Be the change you want to see in the world!

Power Questions:
What do you want to change?

Why not start with yourself! What can you do to initiate this change?

52. Stop trying and start doing!

Just trying doesn't take you anywhere. I'm in line with Master Yoda: Do or do not!

Action Steps:
Make a list of everything you are *trying* to do right now:

Take a decision which things you will actually do and forget the rest.

Power Questions:
How would your life be if you accepted yourself as you are without self-criticism?

How would your life be if you'd forgive yourself and others?

49. Arrive ten minutes early

Action Step:
Try it the whole week and see for yourself if it adds to your life or not!

50. Speak less, Listen more!

Action Step:
Become a good listener! Practice listening. Concentrate on the person in front of you and quiet down that inner voice that comes up with solutions after 30 seconds.

47. Start saving

Power Question:
In which areas of your life can you spend less?

Action Step:
Put 10% of your salary on a separate savings account at the beginning of the month.

48. Forgive everybody who has wronged you

Action Steps:
1. Make a list of everybody that you haven't forgiven:

2. Make a list of everything you haven't forgiven yourself:

44. Smile more!

Action Step:
For the next seven days stand in front of a mirror and smile to yourself for one minute. Do that at least three times a day and observe what you feel.

45. Take a power nap

Action Step: Start power napping.

46. Read half an hour every day

Action Step:
Make a list of 6 books that you will read in the next three months (or faster)! If you don't know check out my webpage for recommendations. **But write that list NOW!**

1. _____

2. _____

3. _____

4. _____

5. _____

6. _____

42. Multitasking is a lie!

Action Step:
Forget about multitasking. Focus on doing one thing at a time and do it concentrated. ALWAYS!

43. Simplify your life

Power questions:
Where do you see excess in your life?

Do you have too many things you don't need or use?

Is your schedule always booked?

Do you have time in your schedule for yourself and the things you enjoy doing?

What are the most important tasks in your day-to-day life (home and/work)?

Which tasks can be easily delegated, automated, or eliminated?

41. Be happy NOW!

Power Questions:
What is happiness for you? (be specific)

How many smiles have you gifted last week?

How many smiles have you received?

Action step:
Remember the moments that made you most happy in your life. Write down at least five moments that made you feel exceptionally great:
1._____

2._____

3._____

4._____

5._____

Re-live these moments with all their emotions and happiness. How does it feel?

39. Let go of the past

Action Step:
What is in your life that is incomplete?
Make a list and work on it! Complete it or let go.

40. Celebrate your wins!

Power Questions:
What will you reward yourself with for your progress so far?
Will you have a Spa day or a nice dinner? Will you go for a walk?

Action Step:
Write some ideas here:

37. The Magic of Visualization

Visualization is a fundamental resource to install experiences.

Action Step:
Visualize your goals as accomplished. Feel them, smell them, hear them. Do this 5 minutes a day for 30 days! Use the book for instructions.

38. What if?

Action Step:
Write a list with all you fears and negative "What ifs" and turn them into positive "what ifs".

36. Adapt an Attitude of Gratitude!

Action Steps:
1) Make a list of everything you have in your life that you are grateful for. Write everything you can think of. (This should be a long list)

2) For 30 days every day write 3 to 5 things that you are grateful for that day into your journal. Before going to sleep relive the moments. Relive the happiness.

34. Take a walk every day

Whenever it's possible go out and spend time in nature. Take a walk and connect with it. Watch a sunset or a sunrise.

Action Step:
Schedule 3 walks in your calendar this week. Then do the same thing next week and the week after. See how you feel!

35. What are your standards?

Action Step:
Write down the following things:
Things you will no longer accept in your life:

All the behaviors you will no longer tolerate from others:

All the things you want to become:

33. Find your purpose and do what you love

Power Questions:
Who am I? Why am I here? Why do I exist?

What do I really , really want to do with my life?

When do I feel fully alive?

What were the highlights of my life?

What am I doing when time flies by?

What are my greatest strengths?

What would I do if success was guaranteed?

What would I do if I had ten million Dollars, seven houses and travelled all the world?

32. The most important hour...

Power Questions:
How will your mornings and evenings look from now on?

Will you get up 30 minutes earlier and develop a little ritual?

What will your last activities be before you go to sleep?

30. Clean out your cupboard

Action Step:
Schedule a weekend and get rid of everything you don't need any more!
SCHEDULE THE WEEK END NOW!

31. Uncluttering and Tolerations go hand in hand

Action Step:
Read the chapter again to see the huge impact of uncluttering!

29. Eliminate everything that annoys you

Action step:
Make a list of all the things that annoy you. In your private live, your job, your house, your friends, yourself etc. Start working on it as described in the book!

28. Face your fears!

Power Questions:

1) What is stopping you from living the life you want to live?

2) Which excuses are you making for justifying to stay where you are?

3) What's the worst thing that can happen if you do what you are afraid of?

27. Do you "have to" or do you "choose to"?

Action Step #1:
Try out this little exercise:

```
I have to _____A_____.
If I don't do _____A_____, then _____B_____ will happen.
And if _____B_____ then _____C_____ and then _____D_____
and _____E_____ and then ____Z_____.

I prefer _____A_____ to _____Z_____ That's why I choose
_____A_____
```

Action Step #2:
Make your list of "shoulds" and let go of them or rephrase them to "I choose to" or "I decide to".

25. Get up early!

Power Questions:
Getting up or hitting the snooze button? What's your decision? It's up to you. How important is a better lifestyle and more time for you?

26. Avoid the mass media

Action Step:
Control the information that you are exposed to. Make sure it adds to your life. Instead of watching trash TV watch a documentary or a comedy. Instead of listening to the news in your car listen to an audio-book or motivational CDs.

Power Question:
What will you do?

24. Say "NO" to them and "YES" to yourself

Power Questions:

Are you living your own life or trying to please and fulfil the expectations of others?

Who and what are you going to say NO to starting NOW?

Action Step:
Make a list of things you will stop doing!

23. Start to get organized!

Action Steps:
TRY OUT these little tricks, as it can change your life! I was there and using the little tricks that follow I turned it all around:

- Spend the first 15 minutes of your working day prioritizing what to do.
- Spend one hour a week for organizing and filing papers
- Spend 15 minutes a day throwing away papers and clearing of your desk
- The last 15 minutes of your working day to go through your tasks from tomorrow. What's important? What's urgent
- Use your email in box as a to-do list. Tasks solved get archived, tasks Perunsolved stay in the inbox
- Emails and tasks that you can do in less than 5 minutes: Do them always right away!
- Don't accept any new tasks until you are in control
- Do the job right at the first time, so that it doesn't come back to haunt you and costs you more time later.

Power Question:
Which of the tricks will you try first?

22. Manage your time

Action Step:

Fill in the blank:
"I don't have time to_____

Power Questions:
What are you going to do next?

Will you insist on the excuse that you have no time or will you start making time with one little thing at a time and experience the change by yourself?

What are you going to do? (Remember it's all about decisions and habits!)

Action Step #2:
Write down 5 things you will start doing NOW!

20. Next!

Power Questions:
What are you taking away from this chapter in the book?

How will you deal with rejection from now on?

21. Avoid energy robbers

Become very selfish on how you manage your energy:
- Eliminate all distractions
- Finish your unfinished business
- Work on your tolerations
- Say good bye to all energy robbing people and relationships etc.

Power Questions:
What are the energy robbers in your life?

What will you do about it?

4) What do you have to have achieved in **3 months** to get closer to your 1-year-goal?

5) What are the things that can you do **NOW** to reach your 3 month goal?
   Write down at least three things and TAKE ACTION!

19 .Write down your goals and achieve them!

Power Questions:

1) How do you want your life to look like in **10 years**? There are no limits! **Go big!**

2) What do you have to have achieved in **5 years** to get closer to your 10-year-goal?

3) What do you have to have achieved in **1 year** to get closer to your goal in 5 years?

18. Honor your past achievements

Action steps:
1) Write down a list of the biggest successes you've achieved in your life!

2) Read them out loud and allow yourself to feel fantastic for what you have accomplished!

Personal and Professional Assets
(Who do you know? What gifts do you have? What makes you unique and powerful?)

1)

2)

3)

4)

5)

Once you know your strengths it's time to strengthen them. Concentrate on your strengths - the ones you have and the ones you want.

Action Step #2:
If you are up for it send an email to 5 friends and/or colleagues and ask them what they consider your greatest strengths! This can be quite inspiring and a true self confidence booster!

17. Know your strengths

You don't have to be good at everything. Focus on your strengths. Remember that what you focus on tends to expand. What are you good at? Time to find out – isn't it? So let's get started:

Action Steps:
List your TOP FIVE Personal qualities and Professional Strengths below:
(What are your unique strengths? What are you most proud of? What do you do best?)

1)

2)

3)

4)

5)

Most Significant Personal and Professional Accomplishments (What are you most pleased and proud of having accomplished?)

1)

2)

3)

4)

5)

Responsibility and liability for it	Respect	Reputation
Risk avoidance	Reliability	Recognition (respect and status)
Service to others	Security	Stability
Serenity	Sophistication	Supervise or teach others
To be competent, to be efficient	Social status	Social position
Truth	To be useful	Transcending, leave a legacy
Work alone	Vocation	Wealth
Wisdom	Work with others	Work under pressure

My top 4 values are:

1) _____

2) _____

3) _____

4) _____

VALUES LIST

Achievement	Adaptability	Beauty
Adventure	Comfort	Commitment
Competitiveness	Control	Cooperation
Communication with others	Creativity	Democracy
Change and variety	Caution	Challenge
Dedication	Distinction	Dialogue
Economic benefit	Enthusiasm	Esteem
Ecological awareness	Ethics	Fame
Economic security	Easy job	Family
Health	Growth	Honesty
Help Society	Help others	Honor
Intellectual Status	Influencing others	Innovation
Knowledge	Humility	Joy
Loyalty	Integrity	Leadership
Meaningful work	Merit	Motivation
Professional development	Nature	Order
Peace at work	Life purpose	Personal development
Religion	Quality	Quality Relationships

What activities are you enjoying most? What kind of moments bring you joy and fulfillment?
What can't you put up with?

Visualization:
Take some time. Close your eyes and relax.
Imagine it is your 75th birthday. You're strolling around in the house. All your friends and family are there. What would you like the most important person in your life, your best friend and a family member say to you? Write it down.

1) Most important person of your life says....

2) Your best friend says....

3) Your_____ (family member) says.

16. Know your Top 4 values!

Ask yourself the following questions:
What is very important in your life?

What gives purpose to your life?

What are you usually doing when you have the feeling of inner peace?

What are you doing that is so much fun that you usually lose track of time?

Think of some people that you admire. Why do you admire them? What kind of qualities do you admire in them?

At this moment in time, how would you describe how much fun or pleasure you are experiencing in your life?

If you could put one fear behind you once and for all, what would it be?

In what area of your life do you most want to have a true breakthrough?

What are you really proud of?

How would you describe yourself?

What aspects of your behaviour do you think you should improve?

At this moment in time, how would you describe your commitment level to making your life a success?

At this moment in time, how would you describe your general state of well being, energy and self-care?

What has been your best work that you have done in your life until today?

How exactly do you know that this was your best work?

How do you see your work today in comparison to what you did 5 years ago? What's the relationship between the work you have now and the work you had before?

In what part of your work do you enjoy most?

What is it that you like least?

What activity or thing do you usually postpone?

What have been your biggest wins in the last 12 months?

What have been your biggest frustrations in the last 12 months?

What do you do to please others?

What do you do to please yourself?

What do you pretend not to know?

15. Know yourself

The first step before changing your life is becoming aware of where you are and what's missing. Please take some time to answer the following questions.

What are your dreams in life?

At the end of your life, what do you think you would most regret not having done for yourself?

If time and money were not factors, what would you like to do, be or have?

What motivates you in life?

What limits you in life?

14. New Habits, New Life!

Action Step:
Introduce 10 habits that you want to change in the next 3 months?

1.

2.

3.

4.

5.

6.

7.

8.

9.

10.

P.S. : It helps to have a visual display! And don't forget to reward yourself for your successes!

12. Focus on what you want, not on what you lack!

Action Step:
Use the following questions to change your focus:

How can I improve this situation?

What can I be thankful for?

What is great in my life right now?

What could I be happy about right now if I wanted to?

Will this still be important in ten years?

What is great about this challenge? How can I use this to learn from it

What can I do to make things better?

13. Watch your words

Action Step:
You can really change your life changing your language, talking to yourself in a positive way and starting to ask yourself different questions. **Why wait? Start now!**
What will you do to improve your inner dialogue?

11. Get comfortable with change and chaos!

Action step:
1) Do something that makes you feel slightly uncomfortable every day.

2) What will you change tomorrow? Your daily routines? Exercise? Eat healthier?

9. Have patience and never ever give up!

Action Step:
The habit of persistence is build like this:
1. Have a clear goal and the burning desire to achieve it.
2. Make a clear plan and act on it with daily action steps
3. Be immune against all negative and discouraging influences.
4. Have a support system of one or more people who will encourage you to follow through with your actions and go after your goals.

10. Learn the "Edison Mentality"

Power Questions:
Have you had any failures in the last years?

What did you learn from it?

What was the positive you got out of it?

7. The importance of your Attitude

Action step:
Think of a negative situation that you had in your life and turn it around. See the positive.

Did you learn something?

8. Perspective is everything

Action Step:
Write down some situations in your life that you thought were negative, but with time you clearly saw that you got something good out of it.

Alternative exercise:
Remember that your limiting belief caused you to feel in a certain way, which caused you to act in a certain way, which gave you a certain result...

1) Write down the limiting Belief

2) Remember the sequence: Belief – emotion – action – result

3) To get a different (desired) result - which way do you have to act?

4) How do you have to feel in order to act differently and get a different result?

5) What do you have to believe in order to feel differently, act differently and get a different result?

Action Step:
To change a belief do the following exercise:
1) Say to yourself: This is only my belief about reality. That doesn't mean that it is the reality
2) Although I believe this it's not necessarily true.
3) Create emotions which are in opposite to the belief.
4) Imagine the opposite
5) Be aware that the belief is only an idea that you have about reality but not reality itself.
6) Just for 10 minutes a day ignore what seems to be real and act as if your wish would be true. (See yourself spending money, healthy etc.)

6. What do you believe?

Power Questions:
What do I believe to be true about myself?

What beliefs do I have concerning money?

What are my beliefs concerning my relationships?

What are my beliefs about my body?

5. Choose your thoughts

Action step:
Don't have any negative thought during the next 48 hours. Block them from the first moment and substitute them by positive thoughts of love, peace and compassion. Even if it seems difficult at the beginning hang in there. It gets easier. Then try 5 days, finally a week.

After one week come back here and note what has changed in your life since you think positively?

4. Choices and Decisions

Power Questions:
Which decisions could you make today to start change?

Will you choose to be more flexible? More positive? Healthier? Happier?....

Action Steps:
1) Write down at least three changes that you want do make today and commit to them:

1 _____
2 _____
3 _____

2) Read Viktor Frankl's book "Man in search of meaning"

What would happen if you stopped suffering in your life and took the decision to change it?

What would you change?

Where could you start?

How would you start?

Action Step:
Write down five things you can do in the coming week to start changing the course and start taking charge of your life?
1.
2.
3.
4.
5.

3. Take full responsibility for your life

Power Questions:
Who are you blaming for your life situation right now?
(Your partner? Your boss? Your parents? Your friends?)

What would happen if you stopped blaming the others for what happens to you in your life?

What would happen if you would stop being a victim of the circumstances?

Is it comfortable for you being the victim?

What benefits does it have for you to be a victim?

1. Are you ready to rewrite your story?

It starts here! Go at your own pace don't get overwhelmed. If you've read the book you know that constant small steps will bring you far.

2. Self-Discipline and Commitment

Power Questions:
Where are you lacking self-discipline at the moment? Be completely honest.

What benefits would you obtain if you had more self-discipline?

What will be your first step to reach your goal?

Write down your plan of action in small steps. Give yourself deadlines.

How will you know you've reached your goal of having more self-discipline in _____?

MARC REKLAU

30 DAYS - The Workbook

This book belongs to:

_____

30 DAYS. PERSONAL WORKBOOK

Copyright © 2017 by Marc Reklau All rights reserved.
Cover design by 22medialab.com
Printed by CreateSpace, An Amazon.com Company

Without limiting the rights under copyright reserved above no part of this book may be reproduced in any form or by any electronic or mechanical means including information storage and retrieval systems, without permission in writing from the author. The only exception is by a reviewer, who may quote short excerpts in a review.

Disclaimer

This book is designed to provide information and motivation to our readers. It is sold with the understanding that the publisher is not engaged to render any type of psychological, legal, or any other kind of professional advice. The instructions and advice in this book are not intended as a substitute for counseling. The content of each chapter is the sole expression and opinion of its author. No warranties or guarantees are expressed or implied by the author's and publisher's choice to include any of the content in this volume. Neither the publisher nor the individual author shall be liable for any physical, psychological, emotional, financial, or commercial damages, including, but not limited to, special, incidental, consequential or other damages. Our views and rights are the same:

You must test everything for yourself according to your own situation talents and aspirations

You are responsible for your own decisions, choices, actions, and results.
Marc Reklau

Visit my website at www.marcreklau.com

ISBN-13: 978-1548318468
ISBN-10: 1548318469

30 DAYS

CHANGE YOUR HABITS, CHANGE YOUR LIFE

PERSONAL WORKBOOK

MARC REKLAU

Made in the
USA
Middletown, DE

77464299R10051